Goldilocks and the Three Bears

by Rena Korb

illustrated by Sean O'Neill

Editorial Offices: Glenview, Illinois • Parsippany, New Jersey • New York, New York
Sales Offices: Needham, Massachusetts • Duluth, Georgia • Glenview, Illinois
Coppell, Texas • Ontario, California • Mesa, Arizona

Once upon a time, a family of bears
lived in a green and leafy forest. These
were no ordinary bears. Dad Bear was
enormous. His bushy head almost brushed
the top of the ceiling of their small house.
Though much smaller than Dad, Mom Bear
was still quite large. (She too was a bear,
after all.)

Dad and Mom Bear had a son named Billy Bear. Compared with his parents, Billy was a little bear. He was only in the third grade. He was also lonely. All of his classmates lived in the nearby town of Woodville and never came to see him after school.

The Bear Family

The bears' house was cheery and bright. At night, Dad Bear sat in his great big armchair. It was made out of a solid tree trunk that he and Billy had found in the forest. Mom Bear's smaller chair was covered in soft green velvet. Of course, Billy's chair was the smallest of all, but it fit him perfectly. Like Dad's chair, it was made of wood from the forest. Like Mom's chair, it was comfy with an embroidered cushion.

Upstairs were the bedrooms. Dad Bear had a great big bed with a thick mattress. Mom Bear had a medium-sized bed covered with a fleecy blanket. Billy Bear slept in a little bed carved out of cherry wood.

One morning, Mom decided to fix oatmeal for breakfast. She scooped it into bowls. Dad had a great big bowl, Mom had a medium-sized bowl, and Billy had a wee little bowl with just one scoop. When Billy tried to take a bite, he made a terrible discovery. The oatmeal was too hot to eat!

The Bear family decided to take a hike. Their goal was to let the oatmeal cool off. Now while they were on their journey, a little girl named Goldilocks wandered by their house.

Goldilocks was just about Billy Bear's age and even went to his school. Although she looked like a princess with her long golden curls, she sometimes acted as though everything in the world belonged to her.

"What's that delicious smell?" she wondered aloud. "It must be coming from this house." She peered through the window and saw that no one was at home. So, she climbed right into the bears' house!

First, she tasted Dad Bear's oatmeal. "Too hot!" Goldilocks cried. Next, she tried Mom Bear's oatmeal, but it was too cold. Then, she tried Billy Bear's oatmeal. It was so good that she licked the bowl clean.

"This must be Billy Bear's house!"
she said, looking at photographs in the
living room. Then she noticed Mom Bear's
collection of delicate glass animals. She
took a bunny off the shelf to get a closer
look.

Then she sat in Dad Bear's big chair.
"Oh, this is far too hard." Then she sat in
Mom Bear's chair. "Oh, this is far too soft."
Then she sat in Billy Bear's chair. "This is
just right," she said. But suddenly, Billy
Bear's chair collapsed beneath her, and the
crystal bunny broke into tiny pieces.

Goldilocks went upstairs and into Dad and Mom Bear's bedroom. She ran over to Dad Bear's bed, climbed up, and lay down to take a little nap. This bed was too hard.

Next, she tried Mom Bear's bed. She felt like she was trying to sleep on a marshmallow. It was simply too soft.

She struggled out of Mom Bear's bed and walked across the hallway. "This must be Billy Bear's room," she said.

Goldilocks saw Billy Bear's bed and lay down on it. It was just right! She stretched and yawned, and in a twinkling, Goldilocks was fast asleep.

Just then the Bear family returned home. Unaware that anyone had been in their house, Billy Bear ran to the kitchen, joyful at the thought of eating his oatmeal. Then they made the discovery.

"What's going on here?" Dad Bear said, racing in. They saw footprints across the floor, drips and drops of oatmeal on the kitchen table, and Billy Bear's bowl licked clean!

"Somebody's been eating my oatmeal," growled Dad Bear.

"Somebody's been eating my oatmeal," cried Mom Bear.

"Somebody's been eating my oatmeal and ate it all up," wailed Billy Bear.

They all turned to each other in shock. "Somebody's been in our house," the bears said.

Dad Bear stood tall and said with a roar, "I can take care of any intruders."

Dad Bear went on a search of the house. "Stay behind me," he warned Mom Bear and Billy. They went into the family room.

"The intruder broke my crystal bunny!" complained Mom Bear.

"The intruder broke my chair!" wailed Billy Bear.

They checked the bedrooms next. "Someone's been sleeping in both our beds," Mom Bear said.

Dad Bear flung open Billy Bear's door. There Goldilocks slept like an angel. The intruder was just a little girl!

Billy Bear recognized Goldilocks by her long blond curls. "Goldilocks, you wake up right now!" he hollered, shaking her shoulders.

Goldilocks opened her eyes.

"What are you doing here?" Billy Bear demanded. "You ate my breakfast, you broke my chair, and now you're sleeping in my bed."

Goldilocks looked at the three faces crowding around her. "I'm so-so-sorry," she stuttered. "I sm-smelled the yummy oat-oatmeal, so I climbed through the window and ate your breakfast. I'd better get on home now," she said. With a rush, she disappeared from the house.

"That little girl must be very lonely," said Dad Bear.

"Lonely?" repeated Billy. "She's just mean."

Mom said, "When people are lonely, they feel sad, but they act mean instead."

Billy thought about that for a minute. He felt lonely too sometimes.

"Goldilocks!" Billy Bear called. "Wait a second!"

Goldilocks stopped and turned around. She twisted her hair nervously between her fingers as she waited for Billy Bear to speak.

"Do you want to come and play with me?"

"Aren't you still mad that I ate your oatmeal and all that stuff?" Goldilocks asked.

"No," said Billy. "I forgive you."

"Wow, thanks, Billy! Let me just go ask my parents if it's okay."

"Hurry back," said Billy Bear.

Later, Billy Bear and Goldilocks took a walk with Dad Bear to look for a tree trunk so Dad could make a new chair for Billy Bear.

At the end of the day, they all ate the special treats that Mom Bear had made: peanut butter and honey bars. Goldilocks said they were even more delicious than Billy Bear's oatmeal. "And my new friend is not too big or too small, or too anything! He's just right," she added.

Bears in the Wild

Wild bears live in North America, Europe, and Asia. Grizzly bears, black bears, and brown bears live in the United States. Bears live alone and rarely travel in groups.

Most bears will eat almost anything: fish, insects, other animals, seeds, roots, nuts, and berries. They also are very fond of ants and honey.

When bear cubs are born, they weigh only about a pound. The cubs stay with their mother for about a year and a half. She teaches them how to hunt, find food, and take care of themselves.

In the fall, bears eat a lot of food. Then they spend the next two to six months hibernating, or sleeping.